MW01381127

Black Background Mandalas to Color

✦ Beardsley Collection No. 4 ✦

by Joan Verch-Rhys

based on illustrations by Aubrey Beardsley

Black Background Coloring Pages - Vol. 1

The 25 black-background mandalas in this book are a different kind of coloring pages. They're a change of pace. They present a different way of looking at negative space -- the spaces between the lines. Also, they can be faster to complete than regular coloring pages, with dramatically different results.

Most of these mandalas will look best with bold colors, and are especially suited to coloring with markers. (As usual, be sure to place a blank sheet of paper between the page you're coloring and the next one, so the ink won't "bleed" through.)

If a coloring area seems too detailed, you can color over it with a black pen. Also, remember that white is a color. It's okay to leave some areas uncolored and white, for contrast.

All of these mandalas are based on the art of Art Nouveau innovator and illustrator Aubrey Beardsley (1872-1898).

At the back of this book, you'll find coloring tips, plus additional coloring pages from other Coloring Group books.

Style Gallery - Samples of 4 of the 25 coloring pages in this book.

Coloring Tips

Here are some ideas to get the most from your coloring books.

Remember Disney's "Frozen"? A single color (monochrome) can create a lovely, calming effect. Try different shades of blue, like an icy blue, a medium blue (or two or three), and a dark blue. Or, you may prefer to try different shades of red, purple, yellow, green, orange... or any color you like.

Crayon box colors can be fun, too. Try coloring with primary colors -- red, yellow, and blue -- for a refreshing, comfortable look. Or, try Mardi Gras colors like orange, purple, and green. (Just be sure to balance them with lots of white areas, unless you want a Halloween-ish look.)

While we're on the subject of white, it's okay to leave any area white. Or, you can fill any area with black, especially if it's tiny. In fact, you could color an entire page with black, white, and shades of grey. The effect can be dramatic!

If you're coloring for fun and relaxation, choose colors that make sense to you, even if they're offbeat... or *especially* if they're offbeat. For an Art Nouveau look, choose all muted colors. For a "psychedelic 60s" effect, choose brights and neons.

Want some extra flair? Doodle inside the design, or in the margins! You don't have to go "Zen" to add a personal touch to your coloring pages. Here are some ideas to use as fillers. Each square includes a few different doodles to inspire you. (You don't have to use them all.)

Basketweave   Ornaments   Concentric Circles   Arches

Spirals   Wavy Lines   Checkerboard   Decorated Hills

Note: Except for the Basket weave design, you don't need to sketch anything ahead of time. Go freehand! You can doodle with colored pencils or markers, or even a regular pen.

For more tips like these, plus free coloring page samples, visit ColoringGroup.com.

(Doodle art by Aisling D'Art)

Turn the page
for samples
from coloring books
by other
Coloring Group members

From Joan Verch-Rhys' first book, *Art Nouveau Mandalas to Color*, Beardsley Collection #1.
(Also available in her book, *101 Art Nouveau Mandalas to Color*.)

From "Pretty Ornate Patterns 1," by Aisling D'Art

From "Coloring Pages of Yesteryear 1," by Aisling D'Art

Made in the USA
Middletown, DE
21 November 2017